SPOTLIGHT ON NATURE

ZEBRA

MELISSA GISH

CREATIVE EDUCATION · CREATIVE PAPERBACKS

Published by Creative Education and Creative Paperbacks
P.O. Box 227, Mankato, Minnesota 56002
Creative Education and Creative Paperbacks are imprints of The Creative Company
www.thecreativecompany.us

Design by Chelsey Luther; production by Colin O'Dea
Art direction by Rita Marshall
Printed in the United States of America

Photographs by Alamy (Simon Balson, blickwinkel, JEAN-FR@NCOIS DUCASSE, fullempty, Blaine Harrington III, JLMcAnally/Stockimo, Nature Picture Library, Steve Proctor), Dreamstime (Christianef, Ecophoto, Lucaar, Saeful Muslim, Michael Nosek), Getty Images (Barcroft/Barcroft Media, nicolamargaret/E+), iStockphoto (MariSwanepoel, Palenque, ZambeziShark), Minden Pictures (Tony Heald/NPL, Anup Shah/NPL, Adri de Visser), Shutterstock (Eric Isselee, Madlen, Smileus)

Library of Congress Cataloging-in-Publication Data
Names: Gish, Melissa, author.
Title: Zebra / Melissa Gish.
Series: Spotlight on nature.
Includes index.
Summary: A detailed chronology of developmental milestones drives this life study of zebras, including their habitats, physical features, and conservation measures taken to protect these striped, hoofed mammals.
Identifiers: LCCN 2018043956 / ISBN 978-1-64026-187-7 (hardcover) / ISBN 978-1-62832-750-2 (pbk) / ISBN 978-1-64000-305-7 (eBook)
Subjects: LCSH: Zebras—Juvenile literature.
Classification: LCC QL737.U62 G574 2019 / DDC 599.665/7—dc23

First Edition HC 9 8 7 6 5 4 3 2 1
First Edition PBK 9 8 7 6 5 4 3 2 1

CONTENTS

MEET THE FAMILY

BURCHELL'S ZEBRAS of Kruger National Park

Kruger National Park covers 7,523 square miles (19,484 sq km) of northeastern South Africa. Elephants, spotted hyenas, African wild dogs, and a variety of hoofed animals roam the grassy **savanna**. Perched high in a knob thorn tree, a tawny eagle watches a scrub hare and prepares to strike. Vervet monkeys chatter in the marula trees, while lions rest below in the shade. In the distance, where the grass is taller, a Burchell's zebra wanders away from her family group.

It is mid-December, the beginning of summer, and a warm evening breeze rustles the tall grass. For 12 months, a baby zebra has been growing inside its mother's body. The time has now come for it to be born. Its mother needs privacy, away from her family, and safety, hidden from the lions. She lies down in the tall grass. Soon, the baby zebra will enter the world.

CLOSE-UP

Vision

Zebras' eyes are set on the sides of their heads. Zebras can see almost all the way around without turning their heads. Their night vision is as good as an owl's.

CHAPTER ONE

LIFE BEGINS

Zebras are related to horses and wild asses. Like their relatives, zebras feed on grasses and other vegetation. They have long necks and heads, powerful legs, and feet with one toe covered by a tough hoof. Zebras are divided into three species and eight subspecies. Grévy's zebras live in arid and semi-arid habitats of Kenya and Ethiopia. The two mountain zebra subspecies live in mountainous regions of Namibia and South Africa: Hartmann's mountain zebras live on the edge of the Namib Desert, and Cape mountain zebras are scattered throughout the southern tip of South Africa. Six kinds of plains zebras, the most abundant species, are spread from Ethiopia to South Africa. Most of them live on the grasslands of Kenya and Tanzania.

KRUGER NATIONAL PARK BURCHELL'S ZEBRA MILESTONES

DAY 1

- Born
- Able to stand and run
- Weight: 75 pounds (34 kg)
- Height (at shoulder): 30 inches (76.2 cm)

FEATURED FAMILY

Welcome to the World

In the tall grass in Kruger National Park, the female Burchell's zebra lies on her side. She breathes heavily. The sun has dipped below the horizon. Darkness washes over the land. After several hours, a male baby zebra is born. The mother is exhausted. She and her foal rest. Just before dawn, the mother rises to her feet. The foal struggles to his feet for the first time. He steps toward his mother on wobbly legs and begins to drink her warm milk.

The gestation period for zebras is 12 to 13 months. Females give birth to a single baby, called a foal. At birth, mountain zebras are the smallest, weighing about 55 pounds (24.9 kg). Newborn plains zebras can weigh up to 80 pounds (36.3 kg), and Grévy's can weigh more than 100 pounds (45.4 kg). Mothers keep their newborns separated from other zebras for a few days. During that time, the foal learns to recognize its mother's stripe pattern, voice, and scent. This way, the foal will be able to find its mother if it gets separated from her. Foals begin eating grass at about one week old, but they also drink their mother's milk for the first 9 or 10 months of their lives.

CLOSE-UP

Living arrangements

Grévy's zebras are territorial. They choose an area of up to five square miles (12.9 sq km) near a water source and defend it from other zebras. Plains and mountain zebras are nomadic.

(3) DAYS

- Leaves hiding place with mother
- Introduced to other zebras

Newborn foals can stand up within 20 minutes of birth. They can run within two hours. Foals can usually keep up with the herd, but adults work together to protect the youngsters from danger. When predators appear, adults do their best to keep foals in the center of the group and then stand in a semicircle facing the threat. If a predator races forward, the zebras run, staying close together to protect the foals. Sometimes zebras fight back, biting and kicking at their attackers.

CLOSE-UP

Digestive microbes

Tiny organisms called microbes live in zebras' stomachs. These organisms help zebras digest the grass, plants, and seeds they eat. The microbes continue living in zebra dung. Foals will eat dung to get extra microbes.

FEATURED FAMILY

First Meal

The foal is one week old. Born with a full set of teeth, he nibbles his first taste of red oat grass and chews it to a pulp. The grass is good, but he will also need his mother's milk for up to a year. Instinct tells the foal that he might get a tummy ache from the grass. To avoid sickness and help his body digest the grass, he eats a small piece of his mother's dung.

NEWBORN FOALS
can stand up within
20 MINUTES
OF BIRTH.

1 **WEEK**

- First taste of grass
- Keeps up with running zebras

CLOSE-UP

Teeth

A zebra's front teeth, called incisors, are used for clipping grass close to the ground. Four pairs of back teeth, called molars, are ridged for grinding up vegetation. Zebras' teeth grow continuously. Constant chewing keeps them from becoming too long.

CHAPTER TWO

EARLY ADVENTURES

Most zebras give birth between September and April, when food is typically more abundant. Zebra foals are born with a woolly coat of brown stripes that are darker on the head, neck, and legs. They have a bushy mane that runs from the forehead, down the back, to the tip of the tail. When a foal is about three weeks old, the mane hairs past its shoulders begin to fall out. The neck mane begins to stiffen, and the tail is left with long hairs only on the end. After about five months, the foal sheds its fluffy hair. Then, within 9 to 18 months, the brown stripes of its smooth, short coat darken to black. Beneath their striped coats, zebras' skin is black.

Zebras are vital members of the ecosystem in which they live. Ze-

3 WEEKS

- Mane hairs on forehead, back, and tail begin falling out
- Mane hairs on neck begin to thicken

5 MONTHS

- Sheds thick, woolly hair on body
- Coat becomes short and smooth
- Weight: 127 pounds (57.6 kg)
- Height: 38 inches (96.5 cm)

bras eat tall, tough grasses that other animals avoid. When they eat these grasses, shorter grasses can grow. Wildebeest, gazelles, and other animals can then feed on the tender grasses that sprout up. Zebras are also important links in the food chain because large predators such as lions, spotted hyenas, and cheetahs hunt them. As a measure of protection, mothers do not allow their foals to stray far. They yip at their offspring to stay in constant contact. Individuals separated from the group are often captured by predators. Foals are especially targeted. Communication is vital to survival in the herd. Zebras bark, snort, yip, and bray to signal each other.

CLOSE-UP

Racing predators

Zebras can run about 40 miles (64.4 km) per hour. Lions can match this speed but only for about 100 yards (91.4 m). Zebras cannot outrun cheetahs, which can sprint at 60 miles (96.6 km) per hour.

FEATURED FAMILY

Look Who's Running

In Kruger, the Burchell's zebra foal is three months old. He nuzzles his mother for milk, but her body stiffens. The foal can sense her tension. The herd has caught a whiff of something on the breeze. The foal opens his mouth. Curling his upper lip, he inhales, detecting scent through his mouth. Suddenly, two lionesses explode out of the grass. The zebras yip wildly and whirl around. The foal moves to the center of the group and runs with his mother and their family toward the nearby river. The zebras splash into the water, and the lionesses give up the chase. Now the zebras must hope they haven't attracted the attention of any crocodiles.

9 MONTHS

- Undertakes first major journey
- Survives lion and hyena attacks

CLOSE-UP

Stripe patterns

A group of zebras is called a dazzle or a zeal. Each zebra has a unique stripe pattern—like human fingerprints. Individual zebras can be identified by their stripe pattern. The type of pattern varies among species and subspecies.

FEATURED FAMILY

Give It a Try

At the height of the dry season, the zebra foal turns six months old. With little grass, the zebras turn to twigs and tree bark for sustenance. The foal watches as his mother peels away a strip of bark from an acacia tree. Then he mimics his mother. Using his sharp front teeth, he strips away a thin sheet of tree bark. He chews it into a gooey pulp that he can swallow.

ZEBRAS BARK, SNORT, YIP, and BRAY to signal each other.

(11) **MONTHS**

- Fully weaned
- Weight: 190 pounds (86 kg)
- Height: 4 feet (1.2 m)

(14) **MONTHS**

- Stripes become black
- Shadow stripes appear

CLOSE-UP

Feeling vibrations

Zebras have excellent hearing and can turn their ears in nearly every direction. They also "hear" through their teeth. As they graze, they feel vibrations in the ground that travel along the jawbone to their inner ears.

CHAPTER THREE

LIFE LESSONS

Zebras live in family groups called harems. The adult male leader of a harem, which typically contains six or seven mares and their offspring, is called a stallion. He protects the members of his harem and leads them to food and water. After a year, male foals are called colts, and females are called fillies. When colts mature, between ages two and five, they become bachelors. They join other young males in bachelor bands. When fillies mature, between ages two and six, they become mares. They may then be stolen by bachelors to form new harems. Zebra foals quickly learn to remain close to their families. If they stray too close to another harem's stallion, he may try to kill them.

To undertake **migrations**, harems and bands join together to form large herds—sometimes numbering in the thousands. When zebras

18 MONTHS

- Powerful kicks used as defense
- Stands as lookout for the family
- Weight: 265 pounds (120 kg)
- Height: 4.5 feet (1.4 m)

2 YEARS

- Full-grown
- Joins bachelor band
- Height: 4.8 feet (1.5 m)

CLOSE-UP

Cooling off

Zebras live in hot climates. They cool themselves by sweating—just like humans. The sweat dries up, cooling the blood just beneath the skin. Zebras sometimes also pant like dogs.

FEATURED FAMILY

This Is How It's Done

The young Burchell's zebra, now a 12-month-old colt, munches grass with his mother. He is now weaned, meaning he no longer needs his mother's milk. He hears excited yipping and looks over his shoulder. Some of the other colts and fillies are rolling on their backs in the dry dirt. He races to join them, falling onto his side and kicking his feet up into the air. He twists and grinds himself into the dirt. Nothing feels as good as a dust bath!

stand or run in a group, their stripes appear to blend together. Predators have a hard time picking out individuals to attack. Zebra survival depends on two things: escaping predators and locating food and water. Water and green grass are scarce in the dry season, which runs from April to October. Zebras compete with other wildlife for limited water sources. In the rainy season, zebras join together to follow the rainfall toward greener feeding grounds. The largest zebra migrations occur in northern Botswana and on the Serengeti Plain of Tanzania and Kenya. Tens of thousands of zebras join wildebeest, elephants, antelopes, and other animals to travel hundreds of miles to reach flooded pans. As the land dries up again, animals follow the receding water.

(5) YEARS

- Fights with rivals
- Steals first mare
- Weight: 700 pounds (318 kg)

Young zebras must keep up with the adults on these exhausting journeys. Predators follow the migrating herds, constantly watching for individuals that fall behind. Zebras can swim but prefer to avoid it. During migrations, though, zebras and other animals must cross swollen rivers as they head toward abundant food sources. Being slow swimmers, zebra foals may find themselves in the jaws of hungry crocodiles. If zebras can survive the challenges of life in such a harsh environment, they can live for 25 to more than 30 years.

CLOSE-UP

Grooming

Zebras use their front teeth to pull loose hairs off each other. This reinforces the bonds between harem or band members—and it feels pleasant, too. Oxpeckers are birds that clean zebras by plucking ticks and insects off their bodies.

FEATURED FAMILY

Practice Makes Perfect

The zebras of Kruger have traveled to Mazithi Dam. Water is abundant, and the vegetation is lush. The colt is 18 months old and about as tall as his mother, though less bulky. Together, the zebras drink from the lake. Suddenly, a black-backed jackal appears from behind a tree. The colt rushes to take up a position at the front of the harem, shielding his younger cousins. The jackal is not a serious threat. It retreats to the water's edge. The colt continues to keep a watchful eye on the jackal—just in case.

ZEBRAS can swim BUT prefer to avoid it.

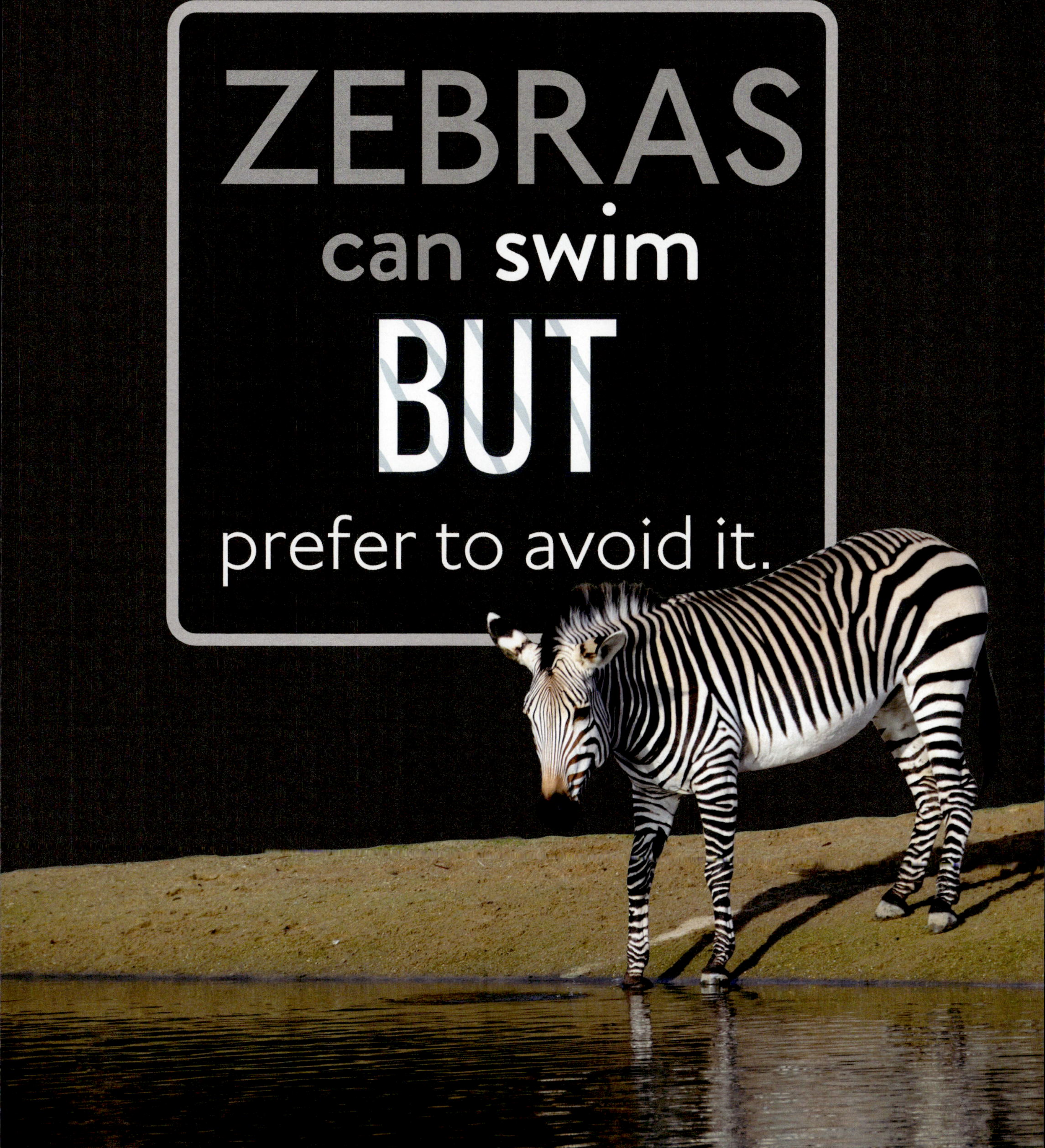

(7) YEARS
- Becomes a father for the first time

(25) YEARS
- End of life

CHAPTER FOUR

ZEBRA SPOTTING

All zebra species once numbered in the millions. Illegal hunting, habitat destruction, and widespread droughts increased by climate change have caused zebra populations to decline. While plains zebra numbers are stable, others have been more affected by human activities. Roughly 25,000 Hartmann's mountain zebras remain in the wild. Fewer than 2,500 Grévy's and about 1,700 Cape mountain zebras remain in the wild. These species and subspecies are **endangered**.

Living in a protected area increases an animal's chances of survival. The Bushmans Kloof Wilderness Reserve near Cape Town, South Africa, is a private preserve. Here, a variety of hoofed animals, including Cape mountain zebras, flourish in relative safety. In recent decades, zebras born at Bushmans Kloof and other private preserves have been moved to Mountain Zebra National Park. The park's 110 square miles (285 sq km) are home to the majority of remaining Cape mountain zebras.

The Grévy's Zebra Trust was established in Kenya in 2007. This organization employs people who live near Grévy's zebra habitat to patrol the areas and teach the members of their communities about the importance of wildlife conservation. The results have been a decrease in illegal hunting and a better understanding of how livestock can share the land with zebras. Zoos around the world also partner with organizations in Africa to study and protect zebras. One program sends veterinarians from the St. Louis, Minnesota, and San Diego zoos to Africa to work with wild zebras. Partnering with WildCare Institute's Horn of Africa Conservation Center, the veterinarians vaccinate Grévy's zebras against anthrax. This deadly disease affects many hoofed animals, including livestock.

Even in northern climates, zebras tend to do well in zoos. Chicago's Lincoln Park Zoo, Canada's Toronto Zoo, and the Smithsonian's National Zoo in Washington, D.C, are home to Grévy's zebras. Hartmann's mountain zebras are kept at the Hogle Zoo in Salt Lake City, Utah; Kentucky's Louisville Zoo; and the Elmwood Park Zoo in Norristown, Pennsylvania. Plains zebras are common in dozens of zoos. Drive-through safari parks allow animals to roam freely, while visitors remain inside their vehicles. Toronto's 740-acre (299 ha) African Lion Safari and Ohio's The Wilds, a 9,000-acre (3,642 ha) park, are such places for zebra spotting. Continued education, combined with research and conservation measures, can help wild zebra populations recover. This is important because the best place for zebras is ultimately in their own wild habitat.

FAMILY ALBUM

SNAPSHOTS

Growing to 9 feet (2.7 m) long and weighing nearly 1,000 pounds (454 kg), **Grévy's zebra** is the largest zebra species.

Hartmann's mountain zebras live on the edge of the Namib Desert. There they climb rocky mountain slopes and sometimes sleep in caves.

At only four feet (1.2 m) tall at the shoulder and about seven feet (2.1 m) long, the **Cape mountain zebra** is the smallest of all zebras.

Burchell's zebra, a plains zebra subspecies, is also called bontequagga and Zululand zebra. It grows up to five feet (1.5 m) tall at the shoulders.

Of all the plains zebra subspecies, **Crawshay's zebra** has the narrowest and densest stripes, which extend across its belly.

Selous' zebra, a plains zebra subspecies, has broad stripes and a typically thinner mane than other zebras.

Grant's zebra is the smallest of the plains zebra subspecies, maxing out at 4.6 feet (1.4 m) tall at the shoulders.

Similar to **Burchell's** and **Crawshay's zebras**, **Chapman's zebras** have brownish stripes, called shadow stripes, between their black-and-white stripes.

The **maneless zebra**, a plains zebra subspecies, is so named because it lacks a mane of hair on its neck.

Each year, **Burchell's zebras** migrate 160 miles (257 km) from Namibia's Chobe River to Nxai Pan National Park in Botswana. They return to the river for the dry season.

The **Grévy's zebra's** narrow head, broad and rounded ears, and white patch above the muzzle help distinguish this species from its relatives.

Cape and **Hartmann's mountain zebras** differ in appearance from other zebras by the presence of a flabby fold of skin, called a dewlap, hanging from the neck.

Zoo Liberec in the Czech Republic breeds **maneless zebras** with its harem of one stallion and three mares. The offspring are shared with other zoos.

WORDS to Know

ecosystem a community of organisms that live together in an environment

endangered at risk of disappearing from the Earth forever

gestation the period of time it takes a baby to develop inside its mother's body

migrations seasonal journeys from one place to another

nomadic having no fixed home and moving in search of food, water, or grazing land

pans dry lakebeds that catch water for part of the year, allowing vegetation to flourish

savanna a grassy, mostly treeless plain in tropical or subtropical regions

species a group of living beings with shared characteristics and the ability to reproduce with one another

LEARN MORE

Books

Beck, Paul. *The Field Guide to Safari Animals*. San Diego: Silver Dolphin Books, 2007.

Caro, Tim. *Zebra Stripes*. Chicago: University of Chicago Press, 2016.

Stuart, Chris, and Mathilde Stuart. *Mammals of Southern Africa Pocket Guide*. Cape Town: Struik, 2011.

Websites

"Grevy's Zebra." Smithsonian's National Zoo & Conservation Biology Institute. https://nationalzoo.si.edu/animals/grevys-zebra.

"Zebra." San Diego Zoo Kids. https://kids.sandiegozoo.org/animals/zebra.

"Zebra." National Geographic Kids. https://kids.nationalgeographic.com/animals/zebra/.

Documentaries

Bailey, Adrian. "Great Zebra Exodus." *Nature*, season 31, episode 13. Hat Creek Productions and THIRTEEN, 2013.

Eicher, Benjamin, and Timo Joh. Mayer. *Amazing Africa 3D*. Los Banditos Films, 2012.

"Zebra." *Nature's Great Race*, season 1, episode 3. BBC, 2017.

Note: Every effort has been made to ensure that any websites listed above were active at the time of publication. However, because of the nature of the Internet, it is impossible to guarantee that these sites will remain active indefinitely or that their contents will not be altered.

Visit

CALGARY ZOO

Home to a herd of endangered Hartmann's mountain zebras.

210 St. George's Drive NE
Calgary, AB
Canada T2E 7VE

LOS ANGELES ZOO & BOTANICAL GARDENS

Grévy's zebras arrived in 2016 as part of a new breeding program.

5333 Zoo Drive
Los Angeles, CA 90027

SAINT LOUIS ZOO

A leader in Grévy's zebra breeding, with more than 30 births in recent decades.

Government Drive
St. Louis, MO 63110

THE WILDS

A variety of African and Asian animals freely roam more than 9,000 acres (3,642 ha).

14000 International Road
Cumberland, OH 43732

INDEX